W9-BTL-787

WITHDRAW
Sno-Isle Libraries

VEGETABLES

BY GEMMA McMULLEN

HEALTHY EATING

CONTENTS

Look out for the underlined words in this book, they are explained in the glossary on page 24.

©This edition was published in 2017. First published in 2016.

Book Life
King's Lynn
Norfolk PE30 4LS

ISBN: 978-1-910512-41-8

All rights reserved
Printed in Malaysia

Written by:
Gemma McMullen

Edited by:
Grace Jones

Designed by:
Matt Rumbelow & Ian McMullen

A catalogue record for this book is available from the British Library.

WHAT IS A VEGETABLE?

A vegetable is a plant or part of a plant that is used for food. Vegetables are usually savoury in taste.

Most vegetables taste best once they have been cooked.

VEGETABLES FROM ROOTS

Some vegetables are the roots of a plant. The roots of plants grow underneath the ground.

Leaves

Stem

Root

Onions, parsnips and sweet potatoes are all root vegetables.

VEGETABLES FROM STEMS

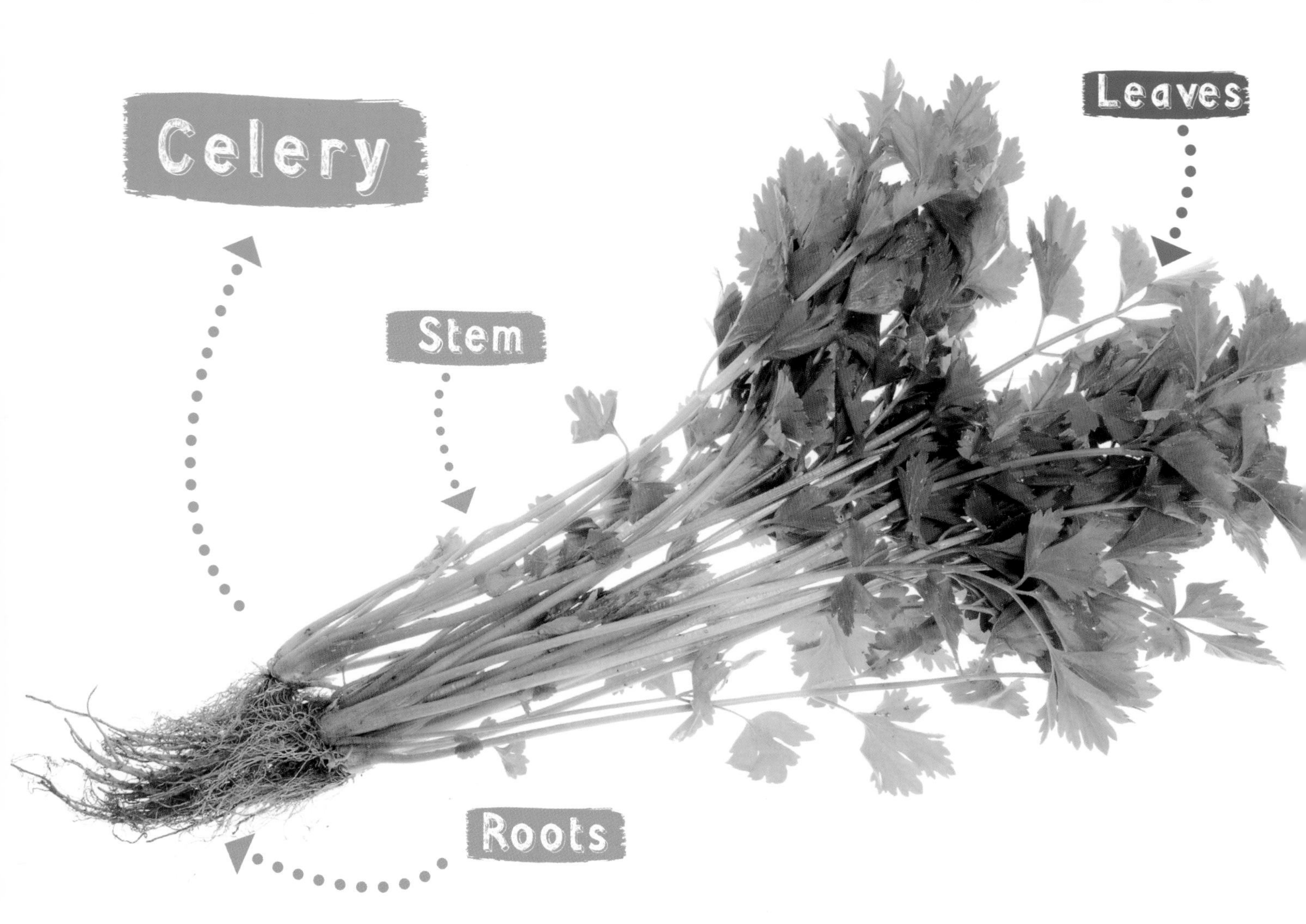

Some vegetables are the stem of a plant.
Asparagus, celery and leeks are all stem vegetables.

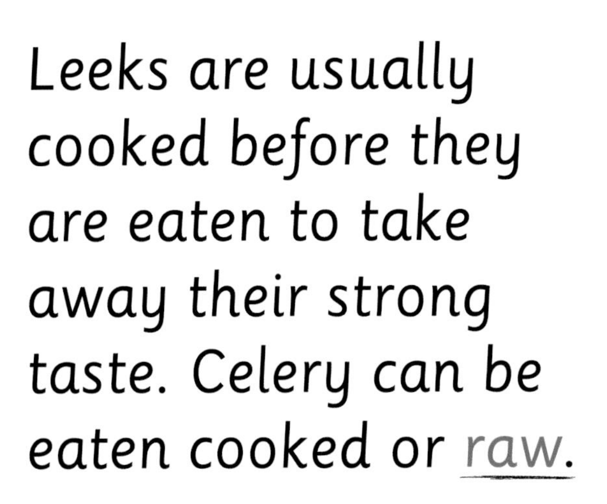

Leeks are usually cooked before they are eaten to take away their strong taste. Celery can be eaten cooked or raw.

Leeks

Rhubarb is often mistaken for a fruit because of its popular use in desserts.

VEGETABLES FROM LEAVES

Some vegetables are the leaves of a plant. Cabbages, sprouts and lettuces are all leaf vegetables.

Not all vegetable leaves are green. This purple vegetable is a red cabbage.

FLOWERS AND SEEDS

That's not all, we also eat the flowers of plants! Broccoli and cauliflower florets are young flowers.

Peas, beans and lentils are actually the seeds of plants.

HEALTHY VEGETABLES

Vegetables are very good for our bodies because they contain important vitamins and minerals. You should try to eat vegetables every day.

It is recommended that we eat at least five portions of fruit and vegetables every day. It is best to eat a variety of fruit and vegetables because they all contain different vitamins.

Raw vegetables contain more nutrients than cooked vegetables.

THE POTATO

The potato is a root vegetable. Potatoes are classed as a starchy food alongside rice and pasta. Potatoes contain carbohydrates.

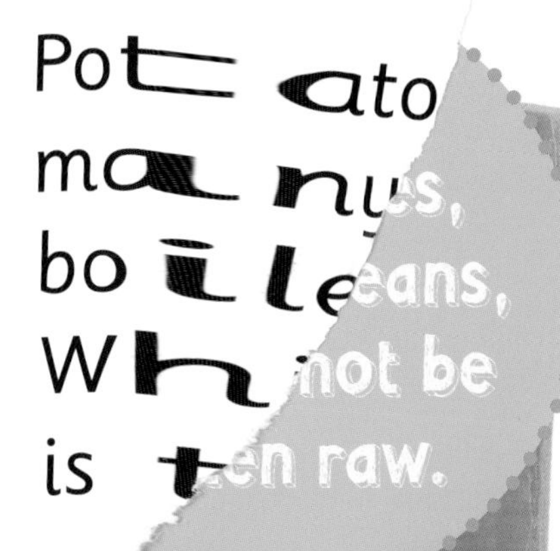

Some vegetables can be
eaten raw as well as cooked.
Raw carrot sticks make
a healthy snack and raw
cabbage is used in coleslaw.

WE ARE NOT VEGETABLES!

Some foods that we call vegetables are actually fruits. This often happens when the fruits are savoury rather than sweet.

Beans, peas, cucumbers, olives, pumpkins and tomatoes are all actually fruits!

FOODY FACTS!

Brussel sprouts are one of the healthiest vegetables, but one of the least liked.

Mr Potato Head was first introduced in 1952.

Onions are very good for you even though they can make you cry.
Eating garlic helps to keep mosquitoes away from your body.

GLOSSARY

carbohydrates
foods that contain sugar and starch to give us energy

nutrients
substances needed to keep the body healthy

raw
not cooked

savory
food that is not sweet

starchy food
food that gives the body energy

vitamins and minerals
substances our bodies need to stay healthy

INDEX

PHOTO CREDITS

Photocredits: Abbreviations: l-left, r-right, b-bottom, t-top, c-centre, m-middle.

Front Cover – Dionisvera. 1 – EM Arts. 2 – Serg64. 3T – sunsetman. 3B – Michael C. Gray. 4 – Serg64. 5 – dariazu. 6 – Casther. 7 – Robyn Mackenzie. 8 – sunsetman. 9T – PhotoEd. 9B – A_Lein. 10 – Candus Camera. 10inset, 22B – Evikka. 11 – Africa Studio. 12 – Michael C. Gray. 13T – oksana2010. 13B – Sergiy Kuzmin. 14 – Paleka. 15 – Elena Elisseeva. 16 – OlegDoroshin. 17L – SeDmi. 17RT – M. Unal Ozmen. 17RTM – Givaga. 17RBM – Villy Yovcheva. 17RB – Peredniankina. 18 – Maksim Shmeljov. 19T – phasinphoto. 19B – Philip Stridh. 20 – Eugenio Marongiu. 21TL – SOMMAI. 21TR – Anna Kucherova. 21BL – Hong Vo. 21BR – topseller. 22T – PAISAN HOMHUAN. 23T – EM Arts. 23B – jps. Images are courtesy of Shutterstock.com. With thanks to Getty Images, Thinkstock Photo and iStockphoto. Thank you to Denise Bentulan for use of her typeface Moonflower http://douxiegirl.com/fonts.